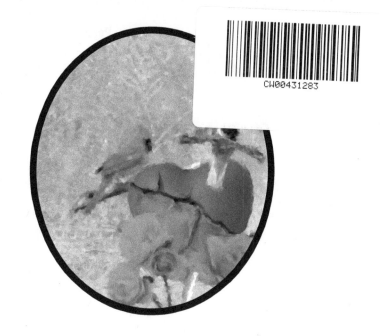

RHYTHMS FOR LOVERS

DEVUN DADDARIO

ANAPHORA LITERARY PRESS

QUANAH, TEXAS

ANAPHORA LITERARY PRESS
1108 W 3rd Street
Quanah, TX 79252
https://anaphoraliterary.com

Book design by Anna Faktorovich, Ph.D.

"A male Northern Cardinal in Columbus, Ohio, USA." Photo by Stephen Wolfe.
17 April 2011.
"A female Northern Cardinal in Florida, USA." Photo by Craig ONeal.
17 November 2013.

Published in 2018 by Anaphora Literary Press

Rhythms for Lovers
Devun Daddario—1st edition.

Library of Congress Control Number: 2017919270

Library Cataloging Information
Daddario, Devun, 1987-, author.
  Rhythms for lovers / Devun Daddario
  96 p. ; 9 in.
  ISBN 978-1-68114-412-2 (softcover : alk. paper)
  ISBN 978-1-68114-413-9 (hardcover : alk. paper)
  ISBN 978-1-68114-414-6 (e-book)
1. Poetry—Subjects & Themes—Love & Erotica.
2. Poetry—American—General.
3. Poetry—Subjects & Themes—Family.
PN6099-6110: Collections of general literature: Poetry
811: American poetry in English

Rhythms for Lovers

DEVUN DADDARIO

CONTENTS

PART 1: The Jaded

(The love that is taught)

The Veil

Who tricked them into
Forgetting how to care?
Numbing their feelings
They've been told not to share

Now it seems that all
Have just stopped believing
In powers of passion
Words can be so deceiving

They all wear a veil
Keeping them from a fairy-tale

They drudge aimlessly
They have but lost resolve
We quietly watch
Once mighty hopes dissolve

There's a careless cycle
Of thick impurity
While they're robbed of
Inner security

They all wear a veil
Keeping them from a fairy-tale

Why have they let go
Of inherent desires?
Throwing them into
Such caustic fires

Each disconnected
From half of their souls
They are chasing standards
That forsake their love's goal

They all wear a veil
Keeping them from a fairy-tale

Who may be so blind?
True beauty does exist
But most chase their views
With the bait that persists

When did we all fall?
And where did we go wrong?
Why allow the weak
Such a hold on the strong?

Hopeful, Lustful

Such standards for companions, what a joke

It's a shared sentiment that forms a bond

Along with other interests and a smoke

It sends ripples through a polluted pond

So now such waters appear to be clean

The inhabitants want new company

But they don't know how to say what they mean

So soon will return their Coventry

An attraction no worse than cosmetic

Internally there are struggles and plights

This, the extent of a cheap aesthetic

Then comes the warning; don't be lead by sight

The reason they still choose mates infernal?

They still see only all that's external

Pleasures and Pity

So late to bed
So late to rise
It's a struggle to
Open our eyes

Their calls for conscience
Are calls we ignore
We won't, they will
And you I adore

With a family
As haggard as mine
Discard the nutrients
Capture the brine

You're the schemer
Idealist me
With much creamer
In your coffee

A threshold pushing
What against? We don't say
A thin shelter
Will only give way

Now aligned
Do we want to feel?
We're unforgiving
With what we steal

That laugh
That yell
You ask
I'll never tell

So early to bed
Never early to rise
Two drowsy smirks
From what we devise

Mixed company
Says that we
Have only met
Coincidentally

Hear The Butchies
And M.S.I.
Pressing my cheek
Against your thigh

Some of your thoughts
Vile like mine
Discard the nutrients
Capture the brine

Unlike the rest
We pray for rain
With an awkward
Hope we constrain

Such habits die hard
And without control
We want the change
But won't pay the toll

That laugh
That yell
You ask
But I'll never tell

Uncaring Reflexes

Well, that mutual fealty
Didn't least long
Did they not hear
The cardinal's sweet song?

That was happiness fleeting
If we've ever seen it
This couple mustn't need it
To keep it they must be it

There's now more confusion
Than ever before
And the imposing thought
Of not trying anymore

Influential comments
From their so-called friends
If called upon to reach
Just how far would they bend?

His armor on the surface
Hides sadness underneath
He's a wildly swinging sword
Who's never known a sheath

When she tries to hold him
He abruptly pulls away
No matter her reassurance
He's convinced she'd never stay

Their painful predicament
Is his own satisfaction
With unknowing precision
He has but one reaction

To derail every story
And shout to the air
That it's not his fault
And she's not really there

But based upon her tales
From each day and age
Along with tribulations
He attempts to gauge

What it is that makes
Her everything she seems
His slightly askew
Perverted little dream

Wilted Roses

Crimson roses tied with ribbon
With laughter wrapped in lace
And empty bottles of Guinness
Strewn all about the place

Slow at first, but soon steadily
Our greed was gaining speed
What once was such a simple want
Became a sudden need

When love presented us the plan
We failed to follow through
We were just too preoccupied
Doing all that we do

If time's taught me anything, it's
That our timing was off
With sore and bitter vocal chords
I shake my head and scoff

Not to dismiss the joyous times
Which others rarely viewed
But because our episode is
Not to be continued

Left behind is a question mark
Both underlined and bold
As I review my old writings
In notebooks growing mold

Wilted roses tied with wire
With remorse soaked in mace
It's so difficult to breathe with
A pillow in your face

So much laughter turned to
Sad, sullen disarray
When an imbecile held his tongue
And watched you slip away

Agony presented the plan
We swiftly followed through
With a war that cannot be won
No matter what we do

Micro-moods of the Macabre Persuasion

When once was absorbed
The richness of all seasons
There's now a deflection
From some intuitive reasons

Where once a man laid
Down at night with royalty
There's now a huge place
That can hold no loyalty

When once were spoken
Words romantic in the cold
There's now tired verbs
Of the turmoil that's been told

Where once a woman
Dreamed of a sparkled paradise
She now kneels to cry
For her husband's vice

When once were smiles
That extended endlessly
There's now only scowls
Which brood aggressively

Where once grew flowers
That held pivotal pedals
There's now just a stem
That always has to settle

When once there was seen
Such pictures titillating
There is now only

Six blind eyes hesitating

Where once was reserved
A golden place so tender
There is now only
Distrust for a whole gender

Baron Time

Look at what we have here, will you?
I must say, I'm not surprised
Given our
Baron time
We are but orphans who belong
To a molested society
We are struggling and starving
With an overwhelming urge to flee
Obliviously on the brink of insanity
And bordering on the sublime
We've gone so far down this hole
And have forgotten how to climb

Listen to the mouths we have here, will you?
I must say, I'm quite irate
At this point
In time
How can you simply believe
What was overheard in a market?
When anyone who is happy
Certainly becomes a target
Woman, I swear, you have some ovaries
To stand there and call me out
On a vague issue from a past
Which you know nothing about

Fathom what has happened here, will you?
I must say, we've clearly
Outdone ourselves
This time
I refused to pull my punches
As you pulled out all the stops
And things become so complicated
Once someone involves the cops
It's rather troubling to forget

It's impossible to make amends
And if what I have heard is true
It seems that all is well that ends

Desolate

He now staggers through these
Desolate streets at night
Passing figures outlined
By a distant streetlight

Propositions are made
Negotiations will fail
Empathetic outcasts
Will hear the vivid tale

Of that pair of hazy
Poor, ill-fated lovers
Who held themselves so high
Higher than all others

He then lies under these
Unwashed bed-sheets at night
While hearing a victim's
Distinguishable fright

From time to time there is
A feint scent of her hair
He pretends she still sits
In that beige, weathered chair

Soon he will sift though these
Broken pieces at night
Hunting down the fragments
While adding to his plight

He yields to current fate
Not learning what it takes
To see his very fate
Is only what he makes

His temper absolves him
Of all of which he cares
But it will not save him
From his future nightmares

Hedonistic Harvest

Primal urges before
A couple bodies explore
Ends with
Testicular
Juices dripping
From cracked, lubricious lips
Descending unto
Silk sheets glistening
Before seeping through to
An emaciated mattress
Many pairs, deceptive and unfaithful
Interlock treacherous fingers as
They glide
Stoned and negligent
Through a vacant park
While gleaming, yellow lights
Cast disproportionate silhouettes
Against a circular pattern
That suggests
Which direction they should take
So many
Lie to one another
They have no shame
While doing so
This goes for older felines
Who climb expeditiously
And stalk
Raw meat in a pretty package
Which will rip from them
Maybe an outdated
Unflattering dress
While
Other eager bodies
Are chained
To mahogany bedposts

After getting their dimpled asses
Smacked
With metal-studded straps
Until blood flows from a pleasurable wound
Then an unwavering
Quiver
Exposes a younger body's
Inexperience and naivete
The skin flushes from the face
All the way down to
The thighs
Which nervously await
To try their many planned ways
Of saturating a mate
In mysterious ravishment
They're longing to succumb
To the invariable thrills
And palpitations
Which they have so often heard about
From every
Leg-spreading, semen-swapping
Flesh-biting
Over-glorified
Unabashed peer
Whom cannot differentiate
Between sex
And self-worth

Ill-Will

Why begin
A journey with denial?
If you're seeking honesty
It will be a while

Overused tricks
Would sway a mood
Diverting the attention
Away from who was crude

Mild humidity
Makes up the air
With a colder shoulder
And the harshest glare

Hateful reactions
Will soon seek higher ground
From heavy mistakes
That were sleeping sound

From every corner
Forgiveness may be sought
But that's only because
Hollow stories were caught

What's the value
Of foolish pride?
Has it helped you sleep?
Has it helped you hide?

Is it too late
To just apologize?
It isn't too late
To change how you rationalize

Will you learn
Some battles are worth losing?
But when you're never wrong
Surrender can be confusing

Especially when
You're told to retreat and shut the door
By the very same voices
That are shouting for your encore

Cellophane Cell

As your eyelids grow heavy
Then hang so low
I immediately know
Where you've chosen to go

Recognizing our unequaled
Undeniable intention
By the symptoms of
Your sudden ingestion

Crush with a lighter
That's pressed over cellophane
Hoping for a solution
That you'll never attain

With a liver screaming
From poisons of yesterday
All those colored capsules
Won't make everything okay

Out of my way, I've gone
Doing all to spell it out
Racking my brains so
There would be no shred of doubt

But you don't listen
To half of what you should
You're too damn restless
For your own good

All the male friends
You think are around you
Their goal is to fuck you
That's all they want to do

You aid your own sickness
While pleading for the cure
This is the one thing
Our fusion won't endure

I wish you'd put down that
Fucking rolled-up dollar bill
I wish you'd put down that
Fucking rolled-up dollar bill

That void wont be filled by
The chemicals in that pill
I wish you'd put down that
Fucking rolled-up dollar bill

Of Consequence and Ambiance

Meshed into the couch for the past nine weeks
Twitching and whispering to my ceiling
Silhouettes dance across a room that speaks
I'm scratching with a head that is reeling
The shadows form a taunting cabaret
Dispersing incoherent dialogue
They keep my abrasive wit locked away
And my thoughts dulled-down in a massive fog
Pretty sounds don't erase ugly actions
Nor will they tell me whom I should consult
Is this a plan of the hidden factions?
I have grown weary of the result
Please return that lively girl's conviction
Not that wasted woman's crass addiction

Streamline Smoke

I wish you were here now
If only to feel
My pulse
It races faster than
A heathen catholic to confession
Whom can't handle fidelity
And blames it upon
Possession
For a few brief and wild moments
You and I were unique
Enthused and inspired
We bounced off every bedroom wall
We would leap onto one another
You would make your rhythmic moves
Then invade my mouth with your tongue
I could grab your sultry curves
Then move my hand
Down
Down, down
Until I couldn't help myself
And lift
Your legs so high
I might have pulled them apart
And locked my fists
Around
Each ankle
There was sensing and pumping
Wanting intense thrusting
Repetitive sounds such as those
Disguised themselves as
Justifiable reasons
While we were influenced
By pharmaceutical manipulation
Occasionally preventing
My climax

But we could push ourselves
To the limit
We would light the ends
Of our cigarettes
Resting in silence
I stared at your face
Made visible by the glow
Of the lamp
That sat on your nightstand
When asked about you
I once said,
"I've never seen such a beauty bathe
In the polluted waters of the concrete jungle
And emerge
Unscathed."

Shudder

You
The queen of social bees
I
The king of apathy
Sitting while paroxysm
Creates our symphony
Stoic though I may be
I wasn't as self-aware
Your enticing essence
Forgive me if I stare
Betwixt unsolved riddles
With personal scenarios
And the rest of mankind?
Who cares where it goes?
Despite all we endure
There is little sympathy
Fewer things are worse
Than needing someone's pity

You
The voice of drunken thoughts
I
The silence specialist
In-bedded in contrasts
With guilty perfectionists
Muscles move, muscles ache
The breaking of the dawn
A cheap, white coffee-pot
An answer for a yawn
Our stagnant arrangement
We need to rearrange
Our standard criteria
Is a verbal exchange
With allies and foes
And suburban rejection

You and I know better
They missed the inception

You
Unlike any other
I
Sardonic just the same
They
All see me shudder as
I still airily hear your name

Lucid, Lethal and Lethargic

Dusty, gray curtains are kept drawn
Randomly stapled to a smoke-stained wall
Which now resembles the color of urine
Thanks to all the chemicals and fumes
To which it has consistently been exposed
Windows are coated with the guts of insects
And thoroughly covered with tin foil
Secured by several layers of duct-tape
You always claimed that it saves on electricity
I never questioned that declaration
On the living room floor
Dozens of my novels
Lie in a clutter
I lost my head
And put my knuckles through the shelf
Upon which those books used to rest
"The Subterraneans" is the only book open
Indefinitely exposed is page forty-five
I replay the unholy hour
When you made your final descent
Down our chipped, concrete steps
The porch light was on at that time
It stays so even now
I smashed the switch so that it cannot be turned off
All I do is change the bulbs
After they burn out
This dwelling
We once shared
Shifts every season
A broom remains untouched in the kitchen closet
The sink is full
Of every oily pot, pan and dish we owned

Spoiled scraps now give off a stench
So fucking fowl
That even the rats have vacated this place
As they fled, I asked them to tell you, "Hello."
If they ever happen to see you
During my periods of unemployment
I kept this place
Completely spotless
It seems rather pointless to do that now
And if cleanliness is
Next to godliness
Then I thank god that I'm an Atheist
How many times did I say
I would fix the hinges on our bedroom door?
Probably about as many times
As we both swore to actually stay sober
I look at the burn mark
On the ugly, yellow couch that you left behind
I remember
When we both got so fucked up
That we passed out
And one of us dropped a lit cigarette
Which caused a mild blaze
We doused it quickly then
Blamed one another
We shouted
We fought
Then stopped, stared and laughed
At the idiocy of our bickering
If only
We could have done that when
It mattered the most
But no
Oh no
We were too defensive back then
Many times
I should have paused and assessed why
I was so impulsive
And out for blood without adequate provocation

But I could
Sure as shit
Compose a three hour monologue
On those situations today
But
What good are my words to fall so graciously
If they have no ears to catch them?
I sometimes stand alone in the hallway
The floor still holds vague imprints
Of your bare feet
From when we used to chase each other
Up and down
Around the entire house
As if we were a couple of giddy grade-schoolers
But it's emptiness always causes an echo
When I repeat your lasting statements
To myself
Watching several moths flutter through
Each and every room
Some stay still for hours while munching on my clothes
Others fall under the television's hypnotic glare
It was on that night as well and I never turned it off
I keep the second season of The Boondocks
Playing on a loop
And wonder if you were as surprised as I
When Bushido Brown was brutally beheaded
During the showdown in season three
That show and a certain Mike Judge creation
Are all that I can stand to view
I can no longer listen to Tripping Daisy
Or 311 without a wave of remembrance
Flooding every atom of my being
But King Diamond's "The Conspiracy" still shrieks
From my outdated speakers
The sound is like a Danish banshee being tortured
You never could stand his voice
And you asked me many times
How I could enjoy it so much but not stomach
The vocals of Robert Plant

Either way
It muffles out the unwavering sound
Of the dripping water from the bathroom faucet
It's still rusty and broken and I'm sorry
I wasn't much of a man
When it came to household repairs
But last week I did unclog the bathtub drain
I found the quandary to be a slimy clump of
Your hair
Tangled, knotted and secreting an unspeakable odor
I put that ball of slime into a mason jar
And placed it on our dresser
While unmoved is the thermostat
The temperature remains at fifty-seven degrees
You always preferred the house to feel
Like an arctic tundra when we laid our heads
To slumber
I haven't eaten and I haven't bathed
I haven't groomed and I haven't shaved
I haven't even thought, at least I think
Everything is just
As you left it

I Know You've Seen Her

She's an esoteric, white-trash fiend
An adamant libertine
A deep-seeded, big city lady
Carrying a flexuous gene
You can't deny her
I know you've seen her

She's the one possessing the talent
To control any crowd
She's the one you always hear
Getting raunchy, lewd and loud
You can't control her
I know you've seen her

The sass and wit that she applies
Is consistently abundant
She's pushy but not obnoxious
With phrases rarely redundant
You can't ignore her
I know you've seen her

Underneath the numerous lights
She stands nominated
For just a single chance with her
Oh, so many men have waited
You can't own her
I know you've seen her

With a bare-legged elegance
She sits upon a stool
With the lighting of a cigarette
The hounds begin to drool
You know you want her
I know you've seen her

She's a stout and sturdy alembic
Dispersing such audacity
That triumphs over anyone's
Unfounded, hapless vanity
You can't restrain her
I know you've seen her

Laughing vehemently at the tools
While ignoring all the fools
Who gawk at the sight of her stride
And are controlled by the rules
You can't surprise her
I know you've seen her

She's her own stunning bible
Of unique ideals
That shift to accommodate
However she feels
You can't define her
I know you've seen her

Everyone in this world has met her
At some point in their life
Whether she made you a man
Or perhaps caused you strife
You can't forget her
I know you've seen her

Know that she once was mine
I knew not her angelic value
But heed my mistakes
So this you will not go through
Because I still love her
And I know you've seen her

Internal Puddle of Sorrow

A head hangs so very low
Beneath a darkened sky
With solitude so heavy
Nothing will comply

Few are they whom can see
When there mourns a brother
Over there, once again
Once again, over another

There are pointless and feeble
Ineffectual attempts
That have continuously
Left only fury contempt

Someone's being dumped faster
Than an over-flowing ashtray
Then being kicked to the curb
Like a mangy, unwanted stray

Several pints of gin will not
Assist with one's vertigo
A Sagittarius should not
Meld with a Scorpio

Peace sought shall never come
When one will only analyze
Everything but their actions
They sadly won't realize

Consolidated senses
Don't probe the environment
But that is what contributes
To the agonizing descent

Suffice it to be stated
Things won't be better tomorrow
Moments slowly drip into an
Internal puddle of sorrow

The Absence of Your Presence

My heart still pounds when I think of you
As if I've just done
A line of ice

Many disregarded reasons
Why my words were kept
So damn concise

Misunderstandings over things
Moot and trivial
In such a flash

When we would oppose one another
The world could see
A massive clash

Of twisted and knotted emotions
Which tried their best to
Find the divine

You would assume, I would shout
Then get tight-lipped
And say, "It's fine."

Blatant hysterics caused my silence
Which in turn caused
Your withdrawal

Which was your own way of protecting
Yourself from every
Destructive call

Turn back the clock to a point in time
When everything seemed
A bit more clear

Perspiring on the porch that summer
A daisy behind
Your ringing ear

Enter the pushers and the talkers
That seemed to make you
So persuasive

And without every being attacked
I couldn't help but
Get defensive

Leading to that tedious walk home
Coming all the way
Back from Dallas

Where I caught sleep underneath a bridge
With a rock digging
In my phallus

Most saw only our exterior
Missing the vibes when
We were alone

Our vicious motions that broke the bed
And the dripping sweat
While you would moan

All of that lingers from our tenure
And sometimes I can't
Fucking take it

My one undeniable talent
It's easy for me
Just to fake it

To play the role of the stoic one
Whom has never had
A heart to care

While really choking on solitude
And consistently
Wondering where

Your head lays when not beside mine
My stomach churns at
Any notion

Of an ugly wretch embracing you
Touching and making
Any commotion

As you were the only one whom could
Ever hope to steal
My eloquence

Dear, if you only knew how I can
Still feel the absence
Of your presence

Ostentatious

To view the one woman so zealously
That everything else simply dissipates
Except for the mood that anticipates
Impending betrayal and jealousy
Alas, you are the one whom made this choice
Wishing and wanting it to bring you mirth
Unabashedly, you knew not her worth
Which you proved each time you raised your voice
Now arrive the regrets so painfully
Over all of your long-lost, severed ties
While all that remains is what surely dies
With judgments calculated steadily
Your detriments come to you gainfully
Waiting for sabotage so readily

I Knew a Girl Once...

Of course, there was
That shiver-inducing touch of hers
At her hand's soft attack
On my chest and my back

Which followed
That unmistakable voice of hers
Drunkenly shouting loud
Vigorous and so proud

Then there was
That enticingly tart taste of hers
Lingering on my lips
With saliva trails on her hips

Leading down to
Those shapely, savory legs of hers
So luscious in their shape
And sometimes bound with tape

Also, there was
That signature aroma of hers
Often trailing from her hair
Wafting here and there

Finally, there was
That intriguing little heart of hers
Beating for our laughter
And against all that came after

Every Other Whisper

Within every other whisper
That caresses in the dark
None of it is genuine
It is all but a lark

Every single reaction
From everyone's intention
Invokes someone from the past
Who is too painful to mention

You're never going to
Shake her
You're never going to
Shake her

All the sights set upon your eyes
All the objects that you touch
Only pull a mental trigger
That reverberates too much

Every piece of art you show
To all the people that you know
Is but an obvious critique
Of how you can not let go

You're never going to
Shake her
You're never going to
Shake her

Initial plans have now become
Merely secondary
Contributing to your horrors
They are but imaginary

Produced and empowered
By all that you infer
From over analyzing
All the fantasies about her

You're never going to
Shake her
You're never going to
Shake her

Time will sluggishly proceed
At the pace of a snail
Friends have grown weary
Of hearing your woeful tale

All you past mistakes will now
Put you forever on the attack
Against every other woman
For you, there's no turning back

You're never going to
Shake her
You're never going to
Shake her

The Coffee Table

The coffee table
Held objects galore
Carved from beach-wood
Gathered from a shore

The coffee table
Heard the conversations
After their waking
And morning salutations

The coffee table
Stood sturdy and strong
Never judging
A horrid song

The coffee table
Chipped and stained
By illogical humans
So deeply pained

The coffee table
Was always there
Throughout everything
A couple had to share

The coffee table
Bared witness to the end
Of a futile message
They both tried to send

Safety Pins and Open Wounds

One day
When he looks back on this
The necessary factors which play a part
In a man's emotional maturity will
Present themselves
As for now
He continues to run in a loop
Of misplaced blame
Continuously in slow motion
Despite the straining of every tendon
See, his cerebral Rolodex of mental photos
Underwent significant expansion when
He met her
And it hasn't dwindled since
She went away
A perpetual slide-show was created
Accompanied by a self-loathing lecture
Of shameful proclivity
While gulping the original caffeinated drink
That is the true nectar of the gods
Subtle yet forceful assistance will be required
For him to break
Subconscious, aggressive habits
Which only exist
Because of his
Exposure to an uncaring, disgusting, maternal backdrop

The Twisted Dichotomy

Here he is
Where he's always been
Where always he shall be

Shaking hands with
Different occupants
Causing the dystrophy

There she was
Not so long ago
Just yearning for his touch

Now she keeps
His symbolism
Inside an antique hutch

There they go
Those that fell from grace
Then quickly quit the game

Locked away
Their toys and tools to
Wallow in their shame

Here you are
Where you've always been
Where always you shall be

Until you learn
The nature of love's
Twisted dichotomy

PART 2: The Faded

(The love that is learned)

Answer in Reverence

Honor my rhymes
Love my prose
Ponder deeply
These questions I pose
Are you honest with yourselves, my Sisters and Brothers
While you adamantly demand only truth from all others?
To all of your partners, are your intentions fully exposed?
When you view the opposite sex, is a promise indisposed?
Has your entire being been invested from the start?
How sacred is the vow, "Till death do you part"?
With your god as your witness, you complete the ritual
But are you sure the faithfulness is mutual?
Can you both handle the promise of monogamy?
Do you feel a constant urge to engage in polygamy?
If such commitment is too great, then why even commit?
Why would anyone lie and cheat when they could just quit?
Are you all cowards whom can't handle true love
Even though you sent prayers for such up above?
Is it worse to be alone than it is to pretend?
Are you ready for this? With Mother Nature you contend
How many rounds have been lost against another's skin?
How many time have you been guilty of unoriginal sin?
Are your adulterous acts caused by that which can't exist?
Does a phantom take the blame when you're too weak to resist?
Can you stop playing the victim of your self-imposed curse?
A love never known or a love wasted, which is worse?
Do you know the difference between indulgence and compulsion?
Are your shameful exploits leaving you with regret and revulsion?
Will a soft willingness be forever poisoned by deception?
Has this lengthy charade shattered everyone's loving perception?
Do you think this is a game for you to manipulate and charm?
Do you think playing with emotions has no lasting harm?
You will understand this is an eternal war of truth and lies
Once your very own weapons deploy the ultimate surprise!

An Emerging Eclecticism

And so, without a movement to be made
Walls have crumbled and sentries have fled
Then your indoctrination starts to fade
With the structure stormed and the ruler dead
Momentously, the veil can be lifted
Amongst heathens your faith can be restored
Once the great hindering has been shifted
This unknowingly of your own accord
The sun will blacken out then shine so bright
That it hurts your feeble, atrophied eyes
Congratulations, you have won this fight
Now simmer in the moment your pain dies
Comes now, the dawn, your heart will awaken
To the truths of which you've been mistaken

The Template

Ah, now you have embraced ascendancy
By admitting your most repugnant fault
Now you shall see without discrepancy
That your merit has begun to exalt
With its rising, realizations are made
What's the template for what you know as love?
Do you now see how they have all been played?
Where came the basis for what you dream of?
Are you aware of whom you are seeking?
How did this concept even come to be?
What's the worth of all you've been keeping?
Do you believe in what you cannot see?
Why does one attract the souls that they do?
Truth be told, you attract what dwells in you

Ode to a Cherished Road

Won't you take a couple seconds and pause
Knowing the answer is retribution?
If the solution is also the cause
And the cause is you, what's the solution?
Let go of all that you are which is pensive
Discontinue what abets your abuse
All which hinders your forgiveness, divorce
Let the words you speak be sensitive
Remember that everything can be a muse
So, always you tread on this supreme course

Know That Now

Mistakes are imperative
So that all may learn
How to approach the new
When given another turn

If weak are the many
Then strong are the few
That learn from experience
Who they are through and through

Happy is the man whom
Understands the cause of things
It helps to see the riches
That this universe brings

We could have sat
We could have talked it out
But swallowing my pride
Left a taste too stout

To me ex-lover
You know who you are
If you change your mind
I am not very far

To the one person
Who somehow got away
What would you say
If you saw me today?

To the one, the only one
If you can hear me somehow
The fault lies with me
I know that now

Until You Return to Me

Many things have I learned, each in due time
One of them is a certain acceptance
Of the paths required to reach my prime
Mentally, this has spared me grievance
It matters not if we're on the same page
As long as we're reading the same story
You should know I've been appointed by Brage
To restore language to all it's glory
So if you have plans to soon execute
Then with the greatest might, follow them through
You have my support without a dispute
If it's indifference that remains in you
Then by all means, seek out your certainty
I'll wait here until you return to me

Three for Serendipity

The first soul was sent
During his most vital teenage years
She showed him that he needed not
The approval of his peers

His practice of commitment
And his learning of appreciation
Began their infant stages
Before the first degradation

Over half a decade came to pass
As did his several other pairings
But those expendable bodies
Were not of the sacred, soul-sharing

Sent next was the second soul
When the time had come
Her purpose being to make him wonder
Where her confidence was from

Her sudden arrival and attraction
It was but a question ongoing
This was to prevent his acceptance
Of the genuine traits she was showing

Blessed was she with a unique inflection
Along with experience and charm
This heightened his capacity to love
Before he caused them both great harm

It was necessary to darken his views
So that he may better see the light
But the next phase was up to him
He had to do what was right

And so he did and so shall we
And when he says it, so shall it be
When he's given the final soul
Of the serendipitous three

He has persevered, the time is nigh
A young man has earned his right to fly
Send the feminine soul that shall never lie
Let the two become one and hear them cry!

Mephitic

Distrustful and weary were they
Upon the initial meeting
Denying such massive intrigue
From their jaded hearts beating

Thrust into a situation
In a place they didn't understand
While unbeknownst to them
The universe held them in its plan

The more they rejected the call
Ah, the louder it became
And the time was drawing closer
For them to never be the same

Eventually finding comfort through
Respecting one another's presence
While gradually transforming
Into a mutual resonance

Steadily and assuredly
She helped him face his greatest fears
And with his glowing confidence
He strongly lead her past her tears

Months passed and he learned her hobby
Was studying the human mind
Her knowledge he wanted to believe
But his judgment was a bit unkind

Until one windy summer's eve
With boredom he called her out
To test her claims about one's brain
And settle a lingering doubt

Showing him a detailed picture
Her eyes lit up with a monologue
And he stared, immersed in wonder
During a pivotal dialogue

She described the parts she knew
Telling of what each was used for
Tracing her fingers around his head
He sat facing her on the floor

Something on the graph caught his eye
He asked her of its purpose
She told him and his imagination
Dove deep beneath the surface

In a flash he had a theory
Which he had no chance to declare
Suddenly, tremendously
Their heads turned, locked in a stare

Now there is no written language
To convey their experience
Witnessing a world locked away
With a once forbidden clearance

Their essence became unified
They felt perfect synergy
They felt the universe within
And found the meaning of energy

Seeing all that was beyond themselves
Becoming acquainted with their true forms
They were given the key to the door
Inside which all sentience reforms

They viewed a window to the past
Where lovers had become so lost
They saw the road to repair where
Anguish and torment was the cost

Then in less than a second
They relived each of their past lives
From their process of creation
Of which their present life derives

They were two strong but battered souls
Vanquished by fear and confusion
But it took them only one night
To shatter the illusion

Of all that they had been taught
And of all which they had been told
And all at once they realized
Their lives had been covertly sold

During their age of innocence
They signed an invisible contract
Forfeiting their a reality
But that night they got it back

They flipped through endless pages
That held their ancient lineage
The tragic downfall of their tribes
And the history of their heritage

For they had been upon this earth
Before even the concept of time
Hers the gift of spiritual guidance
His the gift of language and rhyme

Tears fled fiercely from their eyes
Once they knew what had been taken
From them by man's rampant evil
Which feared the day they would awaken

For it was known that once they had
They would soon awaken others
Giving their elixir of truth
To their Sisters and their Brothers

For only a sip of knowledge
Can start a chain reaction
And once minds are purified
There comes an unstoppable attraction

Romance the Deviants

I know that you know a loneliness
Known by no one else on this plane
I see that you see a unity
Which seems yet impossible to attain

Romance enter into them
Into every woman, every man
Romance enter into them
Show them that they can

I know that you know of a place
With little space left for you to hide
I heard that you heard the others
Sulk in their hope that's been denied

Romance enter into them
Show each pair the other side
Romance enter into them
Let their bruised hearts collide

I know that you know they've counted
On you to be the one they could deceive
I believe that you believe you've given
Your all with nothing to receive

Romance enter into them
Mix their emotions into a bowl
Romance enter into them
Let them save every heart and soul
Every heart and soul!
Every heart and soul!
Every
Heart and soul!

Through Ravishing Eyes

I never believed it could feel so good to be wrong
Rejoicing, I can hear every note of the cardinal's song
My world has melted into a cascading, glowing mix
It's true, no one's dreams are ever too broken to fix

Raise me, envelope me
Make me throw away this disguise
Praise me, develop me
Through ravishing eyes

I'm infatuated with a smile this genuine
I can be anyone, anywhere, just say when
My internal mechanics someone can repair
With this new potential I will now declare

Select me, perfect me
Till I'm the wisest of the wise
Connect me, reflect me
Through ravishing eyes

I never knew how close I was to being born
I recant all of the useless oaths I have sworn
Companionship exists within each and every letter
Keep doing what you're doing, this will only get better

Feel me, kneel to me
For our bond I hold the ties
Heal me, steal me
Through ravishing eyes

Delight in me, fight for me
Against all of which love defies
Write of me, keep sight of me
Through ravishing eyes

Crown me, renown me
Till my protector lets go and cries
Drown me, go down on me
Through ravishing eyes

Can I see you? (ravishing eyes)
I want to see you (ravishing eyes)
Make me see you! (ravishing eyes)
Through ravishing eyes

Ode to Love's Code

It was difficult to disassemble
When I was deaf and blind to what occurred
I was busy with such a preamble
No wonder I hadn't found the password
Each symbol and clue was right in my face
They begged for me to arrange and deduce
Each part of them that had always been there
But with a simplistic and slower pace
I have straightened out all that was once obtuse
So now allegiance to this oath, I swear

So Eloquently

Ah, to write a verse so eloquently
To reach every part of your heart and soul
The locks are now weak and are falling apart
My many words pierce unquestionably
The deepest part of your estuary
With just cause I focus intently
See, I must infiltrate, oh, so gently
And forgo all that is ancillary
To act with a purpose written in stone
While laughing at others whom have no clue
About you and I and all we can do
To speak such a word that it resonates
An undeniable intention shown
With magic that no longer hesitates

Only the Fools

Now, you have found inner-security
Which shows you the affection others need
To them you slink into obscurity
They aren't ready to unearth this new seed
These are the people you once thought were good friends
They now resent your advice to concede
They will hate the message that your claim sends
Their faith in their egos halts their own cleanse
Dismissed is the empathy you display
Quickly bitten is your hand that extends
As you explain, from your help they refrain
Love and kindness will never change the rules
You know who believes that? Only the fools!

A Message for the Males

Soft
Docile
And rather
Emotional
Versus rough
Dominating
And so very
Territorial
Genetics and environment
Could be to blame
Of course, we're equal
But we're not the same
You wouldn't want him if he had
Lips and hips like her
Your beliefs are twisted
And your rationale, a blur
Many differences, outside and in
So would you chase her
If she grew hairs from her chin?
It's in my nature to protect
It's in your nature to nurture
Our genders must get past
The great communication failure
Men scratch their armpits
Like retarded apes at a bar
See, they have no idea
Of whom and what they are
Builders of massive stone constructs
And weapons of such destruction
Amounting to absolutely nothing
To a sensual female's seduction
Relentless and unwavering we can be
A programmed mission to provide
But we hold little worth
Without the other half by our side

Observe all the spectacles
That men think they have achieved
But they're just arrogant and foolish
Caught by the evil web they've weaved
As sick as it is, parents undoubtedly
Have a greasy hand in this as well
Lean back, listen and observe
And you will be able to tell
If a girl's father was always absent
And that fact screwed with her head
Or if a boy for too long
Slept beside his mother in her bed
We can't deny the numerous charges
Of our primitive, ignorant sexism
Insecurity is why any male
Is threatened by feminism
Which could in turn be the reason
For an explosive cataclysm
Yes, okay, you're right
That's enough with the 'isms'
But know that Freud was a
Self-righteous, coked-up prick
Don't dare claim superiority
Because you possess a swinging dick
The main cause of torment and murder
And ninety-nine thousand guilty cries
Is that hairy, wrinkled sack rubbing
Back and forth between your thighs
And the tightening sensation you feel
Deep inside your bubbling gut
Is what's known as hypocrisy
For the times you branded her a slut
A twat, a cunt, or a dirty-ass whore
Every estrogen-filled organism
Needs to finally even the score
Their eyes have been swollen
Still they manage to pretend
It was their fault, they provoked him
But he won't do it again

But he will
My sisters
Oh, how he will
My sisters
So the next time he gets mad
Before he lets his hand go
Suggest he read thoroughly
A copy of the S.C.U.M. Manifesto
And when you men can't understand
Why she's finally sprinting for the door
Remember all the unjust correlations
You need to take responsibility for
We are the ones who are guilty
Of so much of this world's hate and rape
No more helplessness and silence
A new feminine order is taking shape
All of you big talking, alpha he-men
Can you see the picture any clearer?
Before you blame the other gender
Take a long look in the mirror
Man has for centuries run this world
Then let it rot with injustice seeping through
Enter now, the time to see what
Pairs of hearty ovaries can do
With this monstrosity men have built
And claim they love so much
Because to fix this fucking mess
It will take a serene woman's touch
To shoulder a burden so heavy
Dangerous and demanding
Only a woman has the patience
Tolerance and understanding
That is required for our pitiful race
To finally mature and evolve
Relinquish power to the pussy
And
Problem solved

Off-Beat

They need to get away from here
They need to get lost
Inside of each other
No matter the cost
They will toss around semantics
Like a snowball in winter
And construct wooden secrets
That will never splinter
They will always know victory
Forgetting the word defeat
He's no longer cynical
Since she's a little off-beat

They can run naked and free
Through lush fields every spring
While blissfully accepting
Whatever life will bring
She can study all his reactions
He'll learn all her unique features
They will make indecorous sounds
As unencumbered creatures
They will exude only trust
No lies and no deceit
He'll remain dashingly uncouth
She'll remain intriguingly off-beat

He once was the quiet champion
Until the day she took his belt
She can turn her face away
He'll still know what she's felt
She's intelligent and truculent
Not boorish, it's eccentric
She's proved that there exists
A compliment authentic
He knows his literature

She knows how to be discreet
She can call him maniacal
He will call her off-beat

Ode to Our Abode

Acquiring all tools necessary
To build an eternal structure divine
That provides rest for each emissary
Of the cause that lets the grandest light shine
From each window and every open door
The support gained from the mightiest walls
This home is for all those from the sky
With all rooms protected from roof to floor
They of impurity against it fall
Let them stare in awe, all who pass by

Coalescing Cacoethes

If you're going to look at me that way
Then you better have made some time to stay
Put down the phone and come to me
You know, it's been too long since we
Synchronized our bodies for some fun
So lets show the world how it's done
When you have that smirking implication
I want your oral verification
It's a primitive urge I won't subdue
Which can be satisfied only by you
I'm going to hold you to your claim
That you've got something wild I can tame
So dig your fingernails into my chest
And make me tell you, you're the best
But before you're done screaming out my name
I'm sure that we will need a new bed-frame
I know I drive you utterly insane
When I pull your hair harder than a reign
From every surface, down to the floor
I'll show you just what it means to be sore
No one comes close to your technique
That makes my muscles seize before I peak
After the havoc our ascension wreaks
Don't plan on walking for about three weeks
If your cognizance isn't in a fog
If I'm not panting harder than a dog
And looking like I just lost a fight
Then, my dear, we haven't done it right

Cara Mia

You must know my spoken word's sanctity
I have not trespassed with any other
While my heart belongs still to another
I am a sign that reads 'No Vacancy'
Though I've indulged in random perversions
I wouldn't dare caress another's skin
While between our sheets, it's the greatest sin
I am not more than a 'one woman' person
No one but you can touch me so sweetly
No falsehoods shall ring from these teeth and lips
While drinking from you, exuberant sips
My darling, never shall I turn away
I have committed to you completely
My darling, never shall I go astray

Rerouted Renaissance

A golden sun is setting
So the temperature will drop
We remember we're forgetting
And forget when to stop

They pile the worthwhile
With efforts of reduction
Not futile nor reviled
We're a function of seduction

So cling to me
Just cling to me tonight

Buildings on the south side
Are drenched in the sounds
Of a delightful hysteria
As the engaged make their rounds

Soft-stepping from the fray
Are the surly who survive
They absolve so we evolve
Into one collective hive

So cling to me
Just cling to me tonight

Sycophantic symbols
Guide us along the path
To a rerouted renaissance
From the end of Waco's wrath

Our tribulations may then rust
When our flesh turns to dust
But never give into lust
And know that trust is a must

So cling to me
Cling to me
Just cling to me
Tonight

Alluring Alleviation

Beautifully scarred perceptions collide
Embracing fields, ardent and exchanging
Theories of elation
As well as oxygen
Taking turns condensing
Into splendid particles that re-atomize
As untainted tissue
Tickled by the soft whisper of promises
The spectacle of what they once thought to be vital
To their existence
Forsaking vexations banished to another plane
No power to be gained no lust to be primitively satisfied
Only a mesmeric synthesis to undergo
In order to successfully reproduce
Solidifying a bond with a
Sudden flash
Which births the most coruscating aura
Purple, white and green
Their chemistry
Oh, their translucent chemistry stabilizes
Then imperatively explodes, calculates and venerates
As the various incalculable
Vibrant fragments
Drift along aimlessly as
The process continues

Without You?

He hears the winds
Crying out your name
Longing for something
That can never be the same

The path he once walked with you
He must now traverse alone
Comprehending everything
Majestically, you had shown

It was he you uplifted
After years of being down
You showed him a kingdom
You presented his crown

Illumination you were
In his most dismal hour
Handing him the stones
That would build his tower

He wished you his Queen
With an ego conceded
You gave him everything
That he ever needed

Then you promised him
You were there to stay
But the hand of fate
Forced you away

Now, without knowing why
He must continue
Living and loving
Without you?

Radiant Enchantress

Once upon a solemn autumn evening
You were here and my head wasn't reeling
Envisioning you in a certain year
When all was new, so new, my dear
Guided by instincts and timid dreamers
With everything but intriguing demeanors
What do they know?
What do they know?
What?
Do they know?

Your passions are not for you to ignore
You see that they are necessary for
Aiding the difference inside of you
Have you bitten off more than you can chew?
Or have you made a meal of life by now
By proving them wrong and having them bow?
What do they know?
What do they know?
What?
Do they know?

You're a soul worth more than the going rate
And I know that their bait won't be your fate
Forever my radiant enchantress
With a similar habit to digress
And despite all the tempting decadence
There shall always be your precedence
What do they know?
What do they know?
What?
Do they know?

When You Dream

You, there! Yes, you!
Hold that head of ours up high
Don't you dare believe
She ever told you a lie

Shrug off all doubts
There will be no tears
Was she not the one
Who saved you from all your fears?

When you question
Her memory you defile
Know her promise
Remember it and smile

She saw it all
Even with your every scowl
With all that work
Do you think she would leave now?

Each time you breathe
Within every thought you think
She is with you
Always guiding you in sync

That which happens
Is what must be done
The company of hers
Shall never run

She will be there
With an embrace so sweet
Yes! At the bridge!
When again you two shall meet

She never left
Even so that it may seem
Yes! Forever!
She is with you when you dream

The Language of Lovers

They speak hidden words in total silence
Perfectly timed glares
Can be entire conversations
If one of them shifts their body weight
An important question is being asked
If the other changes their posture
A detailed answer is being given
When a hug comes from behind
A forgotten memory is being recalled
While a hand placed on a right hip
Denotes an
Enthralling promise
A playful push can be a quiet command
But head nods from one to the other
Express a suggestion so sincere
A forceful kiss tells one
That the other is leaving
Caressing the left cheek
Is a reply that declares to one
Where the other will be
Subtle movements keep their secrets
Safely covered from any who may be near
While feint gesticulations
Confuse almost all who would try to decipher
The pair's personal alphabet
Since the vocabulary that they use
Is composed of uncommon
Facial expressions
Average people remain ignorant
And unaware that they're unaware
Of such personal exchanges
Even an elite couple
Whom have been together for years
Would barely recognize
Two beings verbalizing on such a level

And connecting with an ability
So foreign
Only a duo uncannily tuned
Among all hollow imports
Could ever hope to catch
A sultry smirk and reconfigure its intent
To reveal its sender's underlying theme
To be a confident but cautious
Warning
Of whom is approaching the recipient
But even so
The chances of such a thing are
Laughably low
When an outsider is dealing with
A rare form of communication
That only a specific pair can share
It is the dialect of the devout
It is the language of lovers

Their Place of Cathartic Adoration

You must have faith
That one day
You will believe in something
Which you once thought was
Unbelievable
You will see
A moon rise in a woman's eyes
In the blackest time of night
You will hear
A man speak millions of words
With his mouth closed
During three minutes
Of universal silence
You will find
The abilities that exist
Within a belief
That still persists
It's okay to need proof
Before believing in any particular notion
But at the same time
Do not ever forget
That there have always been and always will be
Things in your world
That are incapable of being understood
Or even conveyed with
Your limited senses
This being part of the intrigue
And mystery
Of your journey
But during these travels
Always remember
That you are unique
And loved

Whether that uniqueness
Leans toward love or hate
Is up to you
And you alone
Of course there will be
Those that hurt you
Those that lie
And use your heart
Before they throw it away
In a metaphorical landfill
Full of broken hearts
And severed dreams
Belonging to all of those whom
Loved deeply, initially
But lost
Faith
Because of the actions of those
Who didn't deserve to be loved
By them in the first place
Let the pain brought upon you
By others be a sturdy ladder
Of growth
And emotional maturity
Instead of
A cold crater
That imprisons your trust
Affection and peaceful thinking
Never settle
For someone who doesn't satisfy
And uplift you
This is damaging to
Both souls
Search, search and never
Stop searching
For that one who loves you
For exactly
What you are
You can find
That person who shows you

The powers you never knew about
You are an imperial
Find someone who knows this
And wants to
Strengthen your abilities
Not steal or negate them
There is someone
Who will bring to light
That which you never even knew
You were looking for

Twin Vibrations

It hits as hard as a hammer
But comes with the subtlety of a breeze
It comes with prolonged difficulty
And with such simultaneous ease

It's hotter than any southern summer
But also the coldest winter chill
It's finding the perfect momentum
While standing completely still

Such as it was and is to be
It's such a brilliant emotion
Like an artisan emission
Born from the purest devotion

Oh, it is in itself
A paradoxical contradiction
Hidden betwixt a scintillating
Unshakable conviction

It's something that few can convey
But which so many will deny
Because one can't prove they've seen
Our earth melt into a fulgent sky

And how does one show that they know
What has always been unknowable
How does one express brief control
Over all that's uncontrollable

Because as soon as one claims
That they know that they do
In that instant it merely proves
One has not the faintest clue

And so if the true knowledge is
That we all merely know nothing
How can we define a concept
For that which is something?

Therein lies the situation
With life's ultimate question
Could it be just foolish luck?
Perhaps it's natural selection

But when the seekers of the truth
Meet those whom are the bearers of love
What is left shall become right
And what's below falls up above

Confusion turns to clarity
And the darkness comes to light
All losers become the winners
And the weakest shall find their might

And the universal shall cry out
In the greatest celebration
When two souls are reunited
With each their twin vibration

Reflective Flames

Behold now, that you are Alpha
Know that now, I am Omega
You are the illumination
While I am the penumbra

We see that I am the moon
And that surely makes you the sun
Together we form the ending
Of what has merely just begun

While you control every planet
I command every other star
You hold dear all that which is near
I protect all that is afar

You give birth to that which will live
I arise all that must die
You bring cause to what is laughter
I bring reason to every cry

We've found all that is anything
The others, they call it merit
But all that is sought, we have brought
Only to show and to share it

To all of those who shall listen
Without even hearing the words
Let everyone who is chosen
Now, gather in great herds

Please allow all of them to see
This, our incandescent capture
Of their wily and elusive
Intangible, lustrous rapture

Then let their interests peak with such
Spellbound peculiarity
While at the same time existing
With threadbare anonymity

Hear us declare: "We have been there!"
We often lived as they
Placing blindfolded blame
To all others day after day

And we also had to enact
A long astute observation
In order for us to achieve
Our grandest consecration

It was imperative for us
To solemnly venerate
But first we had invocations
To faithfully articulate

We were forced to come to terms
With all the hatred we commit
And our most viable truths
We had to finally admit

For so long we kept ourselves down
Dwelling on all that we despised
And the pain we felt wouldn't end
Until the night we realized

If us as people, we want to change
In ourselves there must be a fuss
Since the only changing outcome
Forever resides in us

We understand this, you and I
Our own gate to infinity
And with this love, we both shall grow
Till our souls reach eternity   —7/08/2015

OTHER
ANAPHORA LITERARY
PRESS TITLES

*PLJ: Interviews with Gene
Ambaum and Corban Addison:
VII:3, Fall 2015*
Editor: Anna Faktorovich

Architecture of Being
By: Bruce Colbert

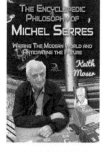

*The Encyclopedic Philosophy of
Michel Serres*
By: Keith Moser

Forever Gentleman
By: Roland Colton

Janet Yellen
By: Marie Bussing-Burks

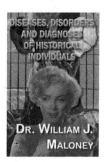

*Diseases, Disorders, and Diagno-
ses of Historical Individuals*
By: William J. Maloney

Armageddon at Maidan
By: Vasyl Baziv

Vovochka
By: Alexander J. Motyl

Lightning Source UK Ltd.
Milton Keynes UK
UKHW01f0648010718

325046UK00001B/2/P